Benjamin Franklin and Electricity

CORNERSTONES OF FREEDOM™

SECOND SERIES

Gail Blasser Riley

Children's Press®
A Division of Scholastic Inc.
New York • Toronto • London • Auckland • Sydney
Mexico City • New Delhi • Hong Kong
Danbury, Connecticut

Photographs © 2004: American Philosophical Society Library, Philadelphia: 10, 35; Art Resource, NY: 16 (Bibliotequ Nationale, Paris, France), 25 (Erich Lessing), 5 (Philadelphia Museum of Art, Philadelphia, Pennsylvania); Benjamin Franklin Institute of Technology/Lufkin Memorial Library: 19; Courtesy of The Bostonian Society/Old State House: 11; Bridgeman Art Library International Ltd., London/New York/Library Company of Philadelphia, PA, USA: 20; Corbis Images: 36 (Archivo Iconografico, S.A.), cover bottom, cover top, 3, 15 left, 21 top, 32, 44 left (Bettmann), 39 (Hulton-Deutsch Collection), 24 (Images.com), 17 (Roy McMahon), 26 (Royalty-Free), 9; Franklin Collection, Yale University Library: 7, 44 right; Getty Images: 8, 12; Hulton|Archive/Getty Images: 4, 30, 31; Mary Evans Picture Library: 22; North Wind Picture Archives: 6, 14 left, 15 right, 23; Photo Researchers, NY/SPL: 29; PhotoDisc/Getty Images: 38; PhotoEdit/David Young-Wolff: 37; Stock Montage, Inc.: 14 right, 34, 41; Superstock, Inc.: 13, 44 center; The Image Works/Science Museum, London/Topham-HIP: 21 right, 27, 45 right.

Illustrations pp. 28 and 40 by Greg Copeland.

Library of Congress Cataloging-in-Publication Data
Riley, Gail Blasser.
  Benjamin Franklin and electricity / Gail Riley.
    p. cm. — (Cornerstones of freedom. Second series)
Includes bibliographical references (p.) and index.
  ISBN 0-516-24240-7
  1. Franklin, Benjamin, 1706–1790—Knowledge—Physics—Juvenile literature. 2. Electricity—Experiments—History—18th century—Juvenile literature. 3. Lightning—Experiments—History—18th century—Juvenile literature. [1. Franklin, Benjamin, 1706–1790. 2. Statesmen. 3. Scientists. 4. Inventors. 5. Printers.] I. Title. II. Series.
  E302.6.F8R545 2004
  973.3'092—dc22
                                            2003023899

CRACKLE . . . BOOM . . . CRA-A-A-CK! The rumble of thunder made Benjamin Franklin sit bolt upright in his bed. He hurried to the staircase and looked at the two small bells hanging across the hall. During a thunderstorm he could usually hear the bells, which were attached to a wire coming from a lightning rod that passed through the roof of his home. When the bells rang, Benjamin knew that the rod and wire were electrified. He could then collect some of the electric charge in a Leyden jar to use later. Tonight was different, though. Right before his eyes, charges so strong that they were visible jumped from bell to bell.

In London, a scientist demonstrates an electrical experiment at a meeting of a scientific society in 1748.

"The fire passed, sometimes in very large, quick cracks from bell to bell and sometimes in a continued, dense, white stream, seemingly as large as my finger, whereby the whole staircase was enlightened as with sunshine, so that one might see to pick up a pin." In this moment, Franklin, a pioneer in the field of electricity, got a glimpse of its future. However, Franklin would not live to see it become a reality.

In the 1740s, the scientific study of electricity was in its infancy. Little was known about electricity, and even less was understood. What was known and understood was not enough to allow electricity to have any practical use. However, electricity was a curiosity. Performers traveled through the American colonies, entertaining audiences by demonstrating the unusual **properties** of electricity.

In 1743, Benjamin Franklin happened to be in Boston and saw one of these demonstrations. He took an immediate interest in electricity and decided to build his own home laboratory to study it. By 1748 he was devoting much of his time to experiments with electricity. Before he was done experimenting, his contributions to the field of electricity were recognized around the world. Franklin was not only elected to the Royal Society of London, England's premier scientific organization, but was awarded its highest award, the Copley Medal. This medal was as important as today's Nobel Prize.

This painting by Mason Chamberlin was made in 1762. It shows Benjamin Franklin seated in his study during a thunderstorm, listening to the ringing of the bells. An iron lightning rod is pictured outside the window.

FRANKLIN'S EARLY YEARS

Benjamin Franklin was born on January 17, 1706, in Boston, Massachusetts. He was the fifteenth of seventeen children. Throughout his life, Benjamin's father, Josiah Franklin, guided young Benjamin in matters of school and work.

Josiah wanted to find a school for Benjamin. He wanted young Benjamin to become a minister one day, as this was a respected and important profession. With this in mind, he sent Benjamin to the Boston Latin School, which would prepare him for college and a career as a minister.

Franklin was born in this Boston, Massachusetts, home in 1706.

Benjamin was eight years old when he started school. He rose to the head of the class with ease. He took to reading quickly. In fact, he learned to read so early in life that he later wrote, "I do not remember when I could not read." Benjamin read whenever and whatever he could, but books were hard to come by. They were expensive, and there were few of them available at that time. Still, Benjamin always managed to find new ones to satisfy him.

Josiah Franklin considered the cost of continuing to send Benjamin to the Boston Latin School and then sending him to college. He had many

As a boy, Franklin read
books whenever he could.

children to provide for, and the expense of the Boston Latin
School and college was great. So Josiah took Benjamin out
of school when he was ten years old and put him to work in
the family store, making candles and soap.

Young Franklin worked alongside his father in the candle shop.

Benjamin's job was to cut wicks, fill candle molds, take care of the store, and run errands. He had no interest in this trade, however. In fact, he hated the work. He found the odor of tallow, the fat used to make soap, disgusting. The job also didn't interest him. Boredom set in quickly.

Instead, Benjamin longed for a career at sea. He often wandered down to Boston Harbor to gaze out across the blue ocean. Josiah was against this idea, however. For one thing, Benjamin's brother had gone to sea and never returned. For another, Benjamin was useful to his father in the candle business.

Josiah wanted to send Benjamin to work at the candle shop of Benjamin's brother, John, but Benjamin would not agree. So Josiah began looking for another trade for his son. Nothing seemed to suit him. Finally Josiah came up with a new idea. He knew that Benjamin was interested in books, so he sent him to become an **apprentice** to Benjamin's brother James in James's print shop, where newspapers were printed.

A view of the harbor in Boston, Massachusetts.

Franklin quickly became a skilled printer during his apprenticeship with James. James began printing the *The New-England Courant* (far right) in 1721.

★ ★ ★ ★

THE PRINT SHOP IN BOSTON

In the 1700s, the practice of apprenticeship was common in America. An apprentice went to work for a master to learn a trade through practical experience. In return, the master provided the apprentice with food and a place to live. The apprentice promised to obey and work for the master until the apprenticeship ended.

This idea did not sit well with Benjamin, who valued his freedom. In addition, James did not make his younger

THE [N° 80

New-England Courant.

From MONDAY February 4. to MONDAY February 11. 1723.

(Reproduction of an old issue of The New-England Courant *with columns of period text, including a passage headed "His MAJESTY's moſt Gracious SPEECH to both Houſes of Parliament, on Thurſday October 11. 1722.")*

LIVING THE GOOD LIFE

Franklin especially liked to read books of a practical nature, those that gave the reader advice about how to get ahead in life. Franklin later came up with his own set of rules to follow in order to live a good life:

1) I will save money until all money owed has been paid back.

2) I will speak truthfully and sincerely. I will not make promises I am not likely to keep.

3) I will apply myself to current business. I will not allow myself to be distracted by a foolish project that could promise quick money. Hard work and patience are the "surest means of plenty."

4) I will speak ill of no one.

brother's life easy. James treated him rudely, gave him orders, and allowed Benjamin little say in how he spent his time.

Benjamin tried to figure out a way to leave the apprenticeship, but it seemed almost impossible. An apprentice promised to work until the age of twenty-one, and Benjamin was only twelve years old. To pass the time, he read books. Benjamin enjoyed reading, but he also loved writing. He was not allowed to write for his brother's paper, *The New-England Courant*, so he wrote poetry and essays on his own.

STRIKING OUT ON HIS OWN

Benjamin Franklin finally decided to run away from his brother and his apprenticeship. He left Boston, boarded a ship, and headed south. Franklin traveled to Philadelphia, where he hoped to strike out on his own and build a new life. He went to work for a printer there and became very successful. He later opened his own print shop. This experience paved the way to the many different roles he would play in the future, including scientist, politician, postmaster, and **diplomat**.

Franklin arrived in Philadelphia in October 1723, hoping to start a new life.

By 1730 Franklin had his own print shop in which he printed a newspaper called *The Pennsylvania Gazette*. In September of that year, Franklin settled down with Deborah Read. Along with the print shop, the two set up a store in the front of their home. He and Deborah sold many things in their store, including pictures, pencils, food, and Josiah Franklin's soap.

POOR RICHARD'S ALMANACK

Almanacs were popular in early America. These books included poems, advice, recipes, jokes, and practical information. In 1732, Franklin began publishing *Poor Richard's Almanack* (right), which included many helpful, practical sayings. Some were Franklin's own. Others were taken from books he had read, which Franklin later adapted to life in the American colonies. Here are some of his best:

- A penny saved is a penny earned.
- Early to bed and early to rise makes a man healthy, wealthy, and wise.
- Hunger never saw bad bread.
- An apple a day keeps the doctor away.
- He does not possess wealth; it possesses him.

Poor Richard, 1736.

AN

Almanack

For the Year of Christ

1 7 3 6,

Being BISSEXTILE or LEAP YEAR.

And makes since the Creation — Years
By the Account of the Eastern Greeks — 7244
By the Latin Church, when ☉ ent. ♈ — 6935
By the Computation of *W. W.* — 5745
By the *Roman* Chronology — 5685
By the *Jewish* Rabbies — 5497

Wherein is contained,

The Lunations, Eclipses, Judgment of the Weather, Spring Tides, Planets Motions & mutual Aspects, Sun and Moon's Rising and Setting, Length of Days, Time of High Water, Fairs, Courts, and observable Days

Fitted to the Latitude of Forty Degrees, and a Meridian of Five Hours West from *London*, but may without sensible Error, serve all the adjacent Places, even from *Newfoundland* to *South-Carolina.*

By RICHARD SAUNDERS, Philom.

PHILADELPHIA:
Printed and sold by *B. FRANKLIN*, at the New Printing-Office near the Market.

A portrait of Franklin at the age of twenty.

BRIGHT IDEAS

Throughout his life, Benjamin Franklin came up with many scientific ideas and inventions. Money did not seem to be at the root of his creations. He even refused to **patent** any of his designs. He felt that he benefited from the inventions of others, so people should be able to benefit freely from his.

In 1741, he began advertising an iron stove he had created. This stove used less wood but produced more heat than a fireplace. It was also less smoky. It became very popular and was later known as the Franklin stove.

Franklin did not patent this design, because he did not want to profit from helping colonists to keep their homes warm.

Some of Franklin's other inventions were also very practical. For example, he made a chair with a seat that turned up, changing into a stepladder. He also hung a cord at the head of his bed that connected to the bolt on his door. When he was ready to go to sleep, he would just pull the cord to lock the door without having to get up again. Other devices that Franklin invented were bifocals (glasses that help people to see both long distances and close up) and the armonica (a musical instrument).

This is a drawing of the Franklin stove, which was later improved by another Philadelphian, David Rittenhouse.

Franklin holds a drawing of bifocals. Today, millions of people wear bifocal glasses to allow them to see better both far away and close up.

Franklin also conducted many scientific experiments. One experiment studied the effect of heat on dark and light fabrics. On a sunny winter day, he laid samples of each fabric on the snow. He later checked to see how much snow underneath them had melted. More snow had melted under the dark fabric than under the light fabric. Franklin figured out that the dark fabric had absorbed more heat than the light fabric did. He put this to use by explaining, "Black clothes are not so fit to wear in a hot, sunny climate."

ATTRACTED TO ELECTRICITY

In 1743, Benjamin Franklin visited Boston. There he met Dr. Archibald Spencer, a scientific entertainer. As part of Spencer's act, Spencer performed an electrical "trick."

Franklin visited Boston in 1743.

To do this, a boy was suspended from the ceiling by silk cords. Dr. Spencer rubbed a glass tube across the boy's feet to create static electricity. Sparks jumped from the boy's face and hands, delighting the audience.

After seeing this performance, Franklin took an immediate interest in electricity. He invited Dr. Spencer to perform his demonstrations in Philadelphia. Then, he bought the equipment Spencer had used for his show and used it to start his own home laboratory. He wanted to study electricity on his own.

During the eighteenth century people knew of only one form of electricity: static electricity. While static electricity formed the basis for entertaining "tricks," few peo-

Rubbing a balloon against your hair creates static electricity.

ple truly understood how it worked. When a person walks across a carpet, reaches for a doorknob, and feels a shock, the shock is caused by static electricity. When you rub a balloon against your hair and your hair stands on end, this is also an example of static electricity.

In order to understand static electricity, it's important to understand what all matter is made up of. Everything around us is made up of tiny particles called **atoms**. In the middle of

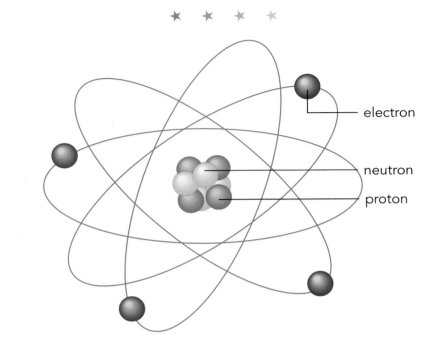

An atom (right), consists of protons, neutrons, and electrons. Protons have a positive charge, and electrons have a negative charge. Neutrons are neutral, which means they have no charge.

electron

neutron

proton

each atom is a **nucleus**. The nucleus contains two kinds of tiny particles called **protons** and **neutrons**. Orbiting around the nucleus are even smaller particles called **electrons**.

Protons, neutrons, and electrons are very different from one another. Protons have a positive (+) charge. Electrons have a negative (–) charge. Neutrons have no charge; they are neutral. The protons in atoms don't move around very much, but the electrons do. Rubbing two objects together can transfer electrons from one object to the other. If an object has more protons than electrons, it is positively charged. If it has more electrons than protons, it is negatively charged. Like the north and south poles of a magnet, protons and electrons attract each other, but electrons repel other electrons. Opposites (a positive proton and a negative electron) attract, or pull toward each other. Two protons or two electrons push each other away. This is what accounts for the interesting properties of static electricity.

If you rub a balloon on your hair to get it to stick to a wall, the balloon picks up extra electrons from your hair and the balloon gets a negative charge. When you place the balloon against the wall, which has the same number of electrons as protons, the extra electrons in the balloon will be attracted to the wall and will stick to it, like a magnet. If you rub the balloon against your hair, it can pick up so many extra electrons that they will actually jump off the balloon onto another object, such as your finger. This creates a spark.

In order to perform more complicated static electricity experiments, Franklin wrote to Peter Collinson, a British scientist. He asked Collinson for materials and information to use in his electrical experiments. Collinson sent Franklin a glass rod and some booklets describing experiments that were being done in Europe. When Franklin rubbed the glass rod with a silk cloth, electrons moved from the rod to the cloth. This gave the rod a positive charge. It gave the cloth a negative charge. Crackle . . . spark! He had created static electricity! Franklin was fascinated. He later wrote to Collinson that he had never before done a study that had so totally absorbed his attention.

Franklin wrote to British scientist Peter Collinson for information and materials.

ELECTRIC BARBECUE, EIGHTEENTH-CENTURY STYLE

Once, Franklin tried to have "an electrical picnic" for his friends. He planned to kill a turkey with an electric shock, then roast it in a "roaster" connected to electrical circuits, like an electric barbecue. But he accidentally let the two ends of the wires touch each other and shocked himself. He was knocked unconscious. "What I meant to kill was a turkey, instead I almost killed a goose," he later said when relating the story.

★   ★   ★   ★

Franklin also created electrical charges with a spinning glass tube. Friends touched the spinning tube and then touched one another. The sparks of static electricity flew. As a result of Franklin's experiments with electricity, he made some important discoveries. For example, he found out that electricity was "not created by the friction, but collected only." This meant that friction did not make electricity. It simply removed electrons from an object. It was at this time that Franklin came up with terms that would

Franklin sometimes used electricity experiments to entertain his friends. Here, some of his friends are gathered around a table playing a game with electricity.

Pieter Musschenbroek demonstrates the principle of the Leyden jar in 1746.

later become accepted in discussing electricity, such as *positive* and *negative*. These terms describe the type of electric charge an object has.

Another discovery Franklin made was that electricity passes through some substances better than others. The substances that allow electric charges to move through them easily, such as metals and water, he called **conductors**. Substances that resist the flow of electricity, such as silk and glass, he called **insulators**.

FRANKLIN'S ELECTRICAL EXPERIMENTS

As Franklin continued his experiments, he figured out how to obtain and store electric charges. For this purpose, he used a Leyden jar. A Leyden jar is a device that early experimenters used to help store electrical energy. It was named after the University of Leyden, Netherlands, where it was

A Leyden jar was a glass jar with metal foil coatings inside and out. It was the first device used for storing an electric charge.

FRANKLIN'S BATTERY

Franklin developed one of the first electric batteries by alternating layers of lead and glass. Lead is a conductor, and glass is an insulator. This early "battery" created electricity through the reaction between the two substances. Electrons are pulled from the glass into the metal, causing a difference in the charges of the two substances. This creates static electricity, which is stored in the device until the experimenter is ready to release it. Franklin's battery was useful for scientific experiments, but it still only produced sparks. The creation of electric current was still far in the future.

Franklin at work in his lab. The large jar on the left of the table is a battery.

invented in 1745 by Pieter Musschenbroek, a physicist and mathematician. The Leyden jar was able to store a charge of static electricity for a time and then release it in the form of a spark or an electric shock. With a Leyden jar, an

* ★ ★ ★

experimenter could store an electrical charge and move it to another place to use.

Franklin had improved the Leyden jar so that more than one charge could be stored in it and those charges would be less likely to leak out. With this version of the jar, more than one spark could be released before the jar needed to be filled again. The jar was covered with metal foil. Water inside the jar was charged with electricity that was inserted through a metal wire. Metal is a conductor, or a material that allows electricity to pass through it. Glass held the charge; that is, it would not allow electricity to pass through it, because glass is an insulator. This is why electricity could be trapped in the jar.

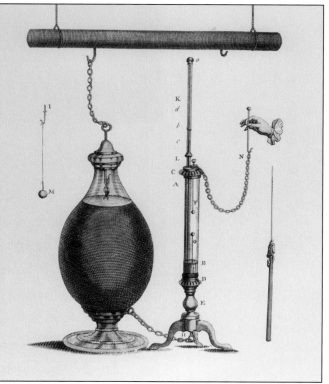

Over time, Franklin used more advanced Leyden jars to carry out experiments. In this particular experiment he showed that a spark generates heat.

Franklin was the kind of person who would invent something he needed if it didn't exist. So when he needed a device to supply enough electricity for him to conduct his electrical experiments, he solved the problem by inventing his "electrostatic machine." This was an early version of an electric generator. Turning a wheel made a glass globe revolve around a chamois cloth, building up a static electric charge in the globe. Knitting needles then made contact with the globe, and the charge passed through the metal needles into a Leyden jar, where the electricity was stored.

23

Franklin performed the first scientific study of lightning, which is powerful enough to damage anything it hits.

GO FLY A KITE

Franklin was now ready to propose his most famous experiment. For years Franklin had watched lightning zip across the sky. He knew its power. He understood that it could reduce the wood of a barn to splinters or take the life of a forest creature or even a human being. He'd seen fires caused by lightning as well.

In 1749, Franklin wrote that he believed lightning and electrical sparks to be alike. Franklin had long suspected that lightning was just a very powerful form of electricity that occurred in nature. Many properties of electricity were already known. For instance, it was known that electricity could pass through metals and other substances. Electricity also had certain magnetic properties that would cause objects to attract or repel each other like magnets.

Franklin wrote to Collinson, the man who had sent him the glass rod for his experiments. He explained the experiment he was planning. Franklin intended to demonstrate that lightning and electrical sparks were the same.

He proposed that a box be built on top of a high tower. A pointed metal rod would be placed in the box so it would extend out the top. At the time, it was already known that electricity was attracted to pointed metal rods. Franklin wanted to find out whether lightning was also attracted to the rod. To do this, someone would stand inside the box during a storm to see what happened.

A DANGEROUS EXPERIMENT

Franklin believed that the person standing near the metal rod would be safe while conducting this experiment. However, this was incorrect. At least one person died due to the lightning strike while attempting a similar experiment.

These are models of various devices Franklin used in his experiments with electricity. A model of a lightning rod on a house is shown at left.

Franklin asked Collinson to present his proposal to the Royal Society in England. In France, a number of people conducted Franklin's experiment with success. The news took a long time to travel across the ocean, however. According to Joseph Priestley, a pastor, scientist, and friend of Franklin's, Franklin grew impatient to learn if his idea was correct. He didn't know about the success overseas, and he wanted to conduct the experiment for himself.

Franklin knew that a kite would reach high enough to draw lightning from a cloud.

In Priestley's account of the experiment, Franklin had planned to use the steeple of a nearby church that was being built. There was just one problem: The steeple was not to be completed for quite some time. Franklin was eager to conduct his experiment, so in 1752 he decided not to wait any longer. Instead, he pressed one of his favorite childhood toys into service—the kite. He knew that a kite could come close to the thunderclouds during a storm.

Supposedly, Franklin built a kite out of silk that was sturdy enough to fly during a storm and not be torn by the wind and rain. A one-foot-long, thin metal rod was attached to the vertical wooden spine of the kite, which pointed toward the sky. The kite string was twine made from hemp, a material known to conduct electricity when it was wet. A brass key was tied near the end of the string to absorb the electricity from the lightning. Finally, a ribbon made of silk, which acted as an

27

According to Joseph Priestley, Franklin asked his son, William, to help with the experiment. Today, some scientists doubt whether Priestley's account is true.

insulator, was tied to the end of the string. The silk ribbon would allow Franklin to hold the kite safely in case any electricity got past the brass key. Once the kite was aloft, Franklin stood beneath a woodshed to keep the silk dry.

Franklin's kite did not actually get hit by lightning that day, but it flew into a thundercloud. It was close enough to the lightning for electricity to flow through the metal rod and the kite string into the brass key. Franklin could see the loose threads of the twine standing up and he could feel the electric shock as he brought his knuckle near the brass key. As a result, Franklin became convinced that his belief was correct: Lightning and electricity were the same.

Being a true scientist, Franklin went one step farther and stored the charge from the key in a Leyden jar. In this way Franklin could be sure that "all other electric experiments be performed, which are usually done by the help of a rubbed glass globe or tube, and thereby the sameness of the electric matter with that of lightning [be] completely demonstrated."

Franklin did not record the details of the kite experiment until four months later, when he published a description of it in *The Pennsylvania Gazette*. In the article, Franklin

This drawing of Franklin's famous kite experiment was based on Joseph Priestley's account of the event.

never refers to himself or his son, William, causing some historians to doubt whether Franklin himself ever conducted this kite experiment at all. Priestley's account, described previously, is the one most people are familiar with today. It appeared in his book *The History of and Present State of Electricity*, published in 1767. Priestley based his description of the kite experiment on conversations he had with Franklin in 1766.

THE MOST FAMOUS MAN IN AMERICA

Word spread about the experiment quickly, and Benjamin Franklin became the most famous man in America. He was presented with a Copley Medal by the Royal Society of London in 1753. Harvard and Yale awarded him honorary doctoral degrees. Franklin's reputation in scientific circles as an **innovator** was established.

Franklin the scientist had demonstrated that lightning is electricity. Franklin the inventor was quick to find an important use for this new discovery: the lightning rod. The idea was simple. A sharp-pointed iron rod several feet long was attached to the top of a building. A wire was then run from the base of the rod down to the ground outside the

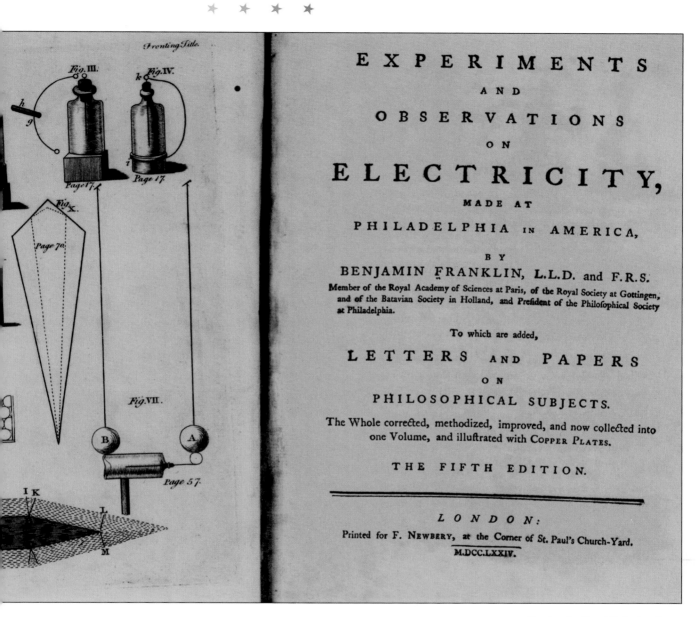

EXPERIMENTS

AND

OBSERVATIONS

ON

ELECTRICITY,

MADE AT

PHILADELPHIA IN AMERICA,

BY

BENJAMIN FRANKLIN, L.L.D. and F.R.S.

Member of the Royal Academy of Sciences at Paris, of the Royal Society at Gottingen, and of the Batavian Society in Holland, and President of the Philosophical Society at Philadelphia.

To which are added,

LETTERS AND PAPERS

ON

PHILOSOPHICAL SUBJECTS.

The Whole corrected, methodized, improved, and now collected into one Volume, and illustrated with COPPER PLATES.

THE FIFTH EDITION.

LONDON:

Printed for F. NEWBERY, at the Corner of St. Paul's Church-Yard.

M.DCC.LXXIV.

building. During a storm, lightning that would normally hit the building would be attracted instead to the rod. The electricity would flow through the rod and harmlessly into the ground, sparing the building from harm.

Benjamin Franklin's book, *Experiments and Observations on Electricity*, was published in 1751.

With the invention of the lightning rod, countless buildings were saved from destruction.

Soon, cities everywhere were installing lightning rods. Countless buildings were saved from being burned down as a result of being struck by lightning. Franklin even installed a lightning rod in his own home—with an added twist.

He wanted to protect his home from lightning, but he was also fascinated by electricity and wanted to observe it and study it as much as he could. The wire of his lightning rod, which ran from the iron rod to the ground, went down through the stairwell of his house. Franklin attached a second wire to it on the staircase outside his bedroom. He then attached small bells to the ends of this wire, about 6 inches (15 centimeters) apart. Between them he hung a brass ball from a silk thread.

During a thunderstorm the ball would swing back and forth and strike the bells. Sometimes it would be repelled by both electrified bells while large sparks traveled between the bells. These bells became known as Franklin's lightning bells. When they rang, he knew that there were charges he could collect in a Leyden jar. He could also observe other properties of electricity.

A MAN OF MANY TALENTS

Benjamin Franklin intended to continue his experiments, but his days as a scientist were drawing to a close. His other skills, especially those as a statesman, were constantly being called upon. In 1751, Franklin was elected to the Pennsylvania Assembly, the governing body that made laws for the state. Then, in 1753, he was appointed deputy postmaster for the northern colonies and did much to improve postal service in the colonies. Franklin left America in 1757 and headed for England. He was sent there as a diplomat. It was his job to represent the interests of Pennsylvanians and others living in the colonies to the British government.

★ ★ ★ ★

When Franklin returned to America, he was asked to join the Continental Congress. This group of colonists was organized to handle the conflict with Great Britain. Franklin helped write the Declaration of Independence. He then

Benjamin Franklin assisted with the writing of the Declaration of Independence.

Franklin was especially good at dealing with people. This skill made him one of our nation's most valuable leaders.

traveled to France to try to convince the French government to provide funding for the colonies' War of Independence from Britain.

Later, Franklin was called upon once more, this time to help with the drafting of the U.S. Constitution. At the age of eighty-one, Franklin became a **delegate** to the Constitutional Convention. He was the only person to sign the Declaration of Independence, the wartime treaty with France, the peace treaty with England that ended the War of Independence, and the Constitution. These four documents were responsible for making the United States of America a new nation.

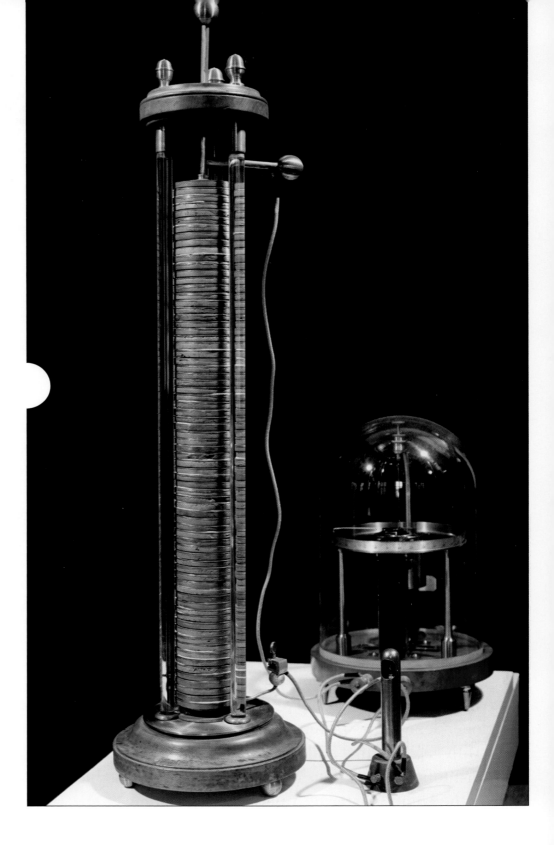

Alessandro Volta is credited with inventing the first battery, shown here, in 1799.

FRANKLIN'S LEGACY

Franklin's scientific investigations greatly advanced our understanding of the nature and behavior of electricity. Franklin was a great inventor and a believer in the practical use of science to make life better. Why, then, was he unable to come up with any practical uses for electricity other than the lightning rod?

He had devised a primitive battery long before the man who was credited with its invention, Alessandro Volta. He had constructed a primitive electric generator to store electricity in his Leyden jar. But two important pieces of the puzzle were missing during Franklin's lifetime. These pieces would later change electricity from being a source of magic tricks to being something practical. Electricity would later provide us with everything from electric light to computers, televisions, and electric motors.

Today, electricity powers our computers, refrigerators, television sets, and other appliances.

Thomas Edison perfected the practical lightbulb in 1879.

The first important advance was learning to make current electricity, or electricity that flows continuously through a wire. In Franklin's time, the only known electricity was static electricity. It was good for creating sparks, but not much else. With current electricity, you could pass electricity through a very thin section of wire and cause it to heat up and even glow. And if you enclosed this thin wire inside a glass bulb and removed the air, it would not burn up right away. Thomas Edison accomplished this almost a century after Benjamin Franklin's study of electricity, and now we have the lightbulb.

The other significant advance followed Michael Faraday's observation that electricity and magnetism are very closely

* * * *

related. A magnet passing through a coil of wire causes electricity to flow through the wire—magnetism causes electricity. Electricity flowing through a coil of wire wrapped around an iron bar causes the iron bar to behave like a magnet. This discovery led to the invention of the **electromagnet** by scientist William Sturgeon in 1825. Electromagnets became important components of the electric motor, and before long, electricity was part of all our lives.

Michael Faraday is known for his pioneering experiments in electricity and magnetism. His studies led to a better understanding of electricity.

Franklin was a lifelong writer as well as inventor. He once said, "If you would not be forgotten, as soon as you are dead and rotten, either write things worth reading, or do things worth the writing."

★ ★ ★ ★

Scientists who followed Benjamin Franklin would owe him a great debt. They took what he had learned about electricity and used it as a basis for making further contributions to the

field. Just as Franklin was a founding father of the United States, so, too, was he a founding father of the study of electricity.

Franklin continued his reading and writing for several years after the Constitutional Convention. He wrote his autobiography, which was never completed, and other works. At the age of eighty-four, Franklin's health rapidly declined. Franklin died on April 17, 1790, at the home of his daughter, Sarah Bache. During his funeral, more than twenty thousand people followed behind his coffin.

Franklin's scientific experiments paved the way to making electricity a valuable field of study.

Franklin has long been honored for his achievements as an inventor, politician, printer, postmaster, and statesman. As a scientist, he is best remembered today for his experiments with electricity. He coined the most basic words of the science vocabulary to express the properties he had discovered. Later scientists, such as Guglielmo Marconi and Thomas Edison, used his ideas to advance their own work in the field. As one of Franklin's biographers, Carl van Doren wrote, "He found electricity a curiosity and left it a science."

Glossary

apprentice—person who learns a trade by working for someone else

atom—the smallest piece of an element that still has the same properties as the element. An atom is made up of a nucleus, a positive electrical charge surrounded by electrons with a negative electrical charge.

conductor—material that allows electricity to pass through it easily

delegate—representative

diplomat—person who represents one government to another

electromagnet—a bar of iron (or other material attracted by magnets) that is temporarily turned into a magnet by passing an electric current through a coil of wire wrapped around the bar

electron—a particle contained in an atom, and having a negative electrical charge

innovator—someone who does things in a new or different way

insulator—material that is a poor conductor of electricity

neutron—a particle contained in the nucleus of an atom, and having no electrical charge

nucleus—the positively charged center of an atom, made up of protons and neutrons

patent—the legal right to be the only one to create or sell a specific invention for a certain number of years

properties—qualities belonging to a specific thing

proton—a particle contained in the nucleus of an atom, and having a positive electrical charge

Timeline: Benjamin

1706	1718	1728	1730	1732	1743

| | Franklin becomes an apprentice to his brother James in a print shop. | Franklin opens his own print shop in Philadelphia, Pennsylvania. | Franklin settles down with Deborah Read. | Franklin publishes the first edition of *Poor Richard's Almanack*. |  |

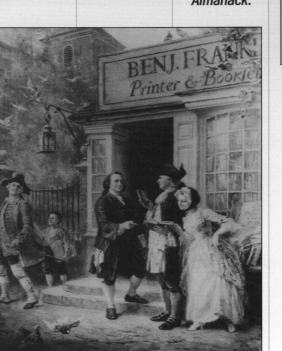

Benjamin Franklin is born in Boston, Massachusetts, on January 17.

Benjamin Franklin visits Boston and meets Dr. Archibald Spencer. After seeing Spencer's electrical "trick," Franklin takes an interest in electricity.

Franklin and Electricity

1752 1753 1767 1776 1787 1790

Franklin conducts his kite experiment.

Franklin signs the U.S. Constitution.

Franklin dies in Philadelphia on April 17 at the age of 84.

Franklin is appointed postmaster of Philadelphia. Franklin is also presented with a Copley Medal by the Royal Society of London in recognition of his work with electricity.

Joseph Priestley publishes his book *The History of and Present State of Electricity*, which contains a detailed account of Franklin's kite experiment.

Franklin signs the Declaration of Independence.

45

To Find Out More

BOOKS

Birch, Beverley and Robin Bell Corfield. *Benjamin Franklin's Adventures with Electricity*. Barron's Educational Series, Inc., 1996.

Cousins, Margaret. *Ben Franklin of Old Philadelphia*. New York: Random House, 1981.

Davidson, Margaret. *The Story of Benjamin Franklin, Amazing American*. New York: Bantam Doubleday Dell, 1988.

Parker, Steve. *Eyewitness: Electricity*. New York: DK Publishing, 2000.

Stevenson, Augusta. B*enjamin Franklin: Young Printer*. New York: Simon & Schuster, 1983.

ONLINE SITES

The Electric Ben Franklin
http://www.ushistory.org/franklin

The Franklin Institute Online
http://sln.fi.edu/index.html

Public Broadcasting Service: Benjamin Franklin
http://www.pbs.org/benfranklin/

Index

Bold numbers indicate illustrations

About the Author

Gail Blasser Riley, a former assistant district attorney, enjoys writing about historical topics. She writes for children and adults and frequently speaks to student audiences.

Riley has taught classes from preschool through graduate levels. Her books, on topics such as censorship, the criminal justice system, natural disasters, and the Miranda ruling, have garnered honors for making complex material interesting and easy to understand.

Riley is the author of more than 350 books, articles, poems, and anthology pieces for Scholastic, Houghton Mifflin, McGraw-Hill, Macmillan, Harcourt, Scott Foresman/Addison-Wesley/Pearson, Steck-Vaughn, Facts on File, and *Newsweek*. Her books have received honors from the Children's Book Council, Young Adult Library Services Association, and the New York Public Library.